Changed Lives

By Joseph Primm

Primms Attitude
http://primmsplace.blogspot.com

CHANGED LIVES

By Joseph Primm

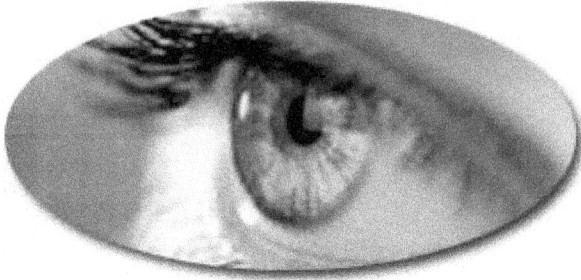

Published by Joseph A. Primm

ISBN: 978-0-578-01674-0

FOREWARD

In the course of life, each generation will ask itself if it has had it better or worse then the other generations. The comparisons are generally hard to make as experience; time and more importantly circumstance dictates what happens. In general, it is just life happening around us. One generation or another is just lucky or unlucky enough to live during that period.

What becomes important is how you work your way through both the good and the bad. Yet there are so many of us that struggle to learn how to change in meeting challenges in our life. Our tendency is to float through life blissfully unaware when things are going good. When bad times befall us, we do as Elijah did in the bible verse of "*1 Kings 19*". We go and hide in a cave wondering if we are worth any more effort.

It is during those times that we need the strength to proceed on to a greater life. We need someone, such as God, to ask us, "*What are you doing here...*" We need to know that we are not the only ones that have gone through a tough time. And we need a glimpse of the possibility that exists for each of us.

The good news is that change can occur. Change has happened in the lives of other people and it can happen in your life. All it takes is finding an open door of opportunity and choosing to walk through it.

As my mother lay in her final hours, she talked of seeing many doors before her and not knowing which door she was supposed to walk through. The answer is that you will know which door is the correct one. It will be the door that opens up and shines with brilliance to light your way.

Read these stories and let them shine on a new path for your life. The door is starting to open for you, make a choice.

ACKNOWLEDGEMENTS

It was not very long before my mother's passing that I decided to write a book about change. It had been about seven months since we first learned she had Pancreatic Cancer. Those seven months were filled with many phone calls and stories of her life.

While many of the stories were ones I had heard several times, it reminded me that so many of us have stories to tell. Each one of those stories had a theme of change. So it was the inspiration from my mother, Rose Primm for which this book was written. To her I have a life time of thanks to give.

There were many everyday and famous folks that I contacted who sent very nice *"thank you, but no thank you"* notes. As I researched and looked for personal stories from other people, I soon realized just how *"personal"* many of these were. Quite a few people held those stories very close and were not at a point in life to share them. Yet I thank all of those that were not ready because I found a deep respect for the stories I did receive.

I really have to thank those that did share their stories with me. Each is very personal and inspiring to others that read them. It is in the sharing and giving of oneself to others that is truly a generous gift to all of us. So thank you most graciously for the gift you have given others.

Additionally, it is the support of my Pastors, Dean and Jill Sweetman; support of my church, Christian City Church – Atlanta; the never ending support of friends and family members that kept me moving forward with this book.

There is also the support of my eight children and my loving wife Laura which remain the inspiration that guides me.

Thank you to the readers, I truly hope you find enjoyment and inspiration in each of the stories before you.

Changed Lives

Introduction

When I started out to write this book, there were so many ways I could have taken the story line. I thought of telling my life's story and how each point along its path was a lesson to teach others. I even thought of creating a series of short stories that each was a lesson within itself. So what kind of story should be written then?

The work of a writer is not something that I would profess to fully understand. I do not consider myself in the same league. The world's great writers are able to weave a tale which takes you on a journey. It pulls you in from the first pages, allowing you to become part of the story as an invited guest.

Each of us will read a story like that and find ourselves wrapping much of whom we are into it. In the end as the story completes, we have hopefully learned something new. Maybe we learned something about who we are. Or maybe we take a piece of the story and apply it to our own life.

These lessons of lives changed are here to allow you to enter the lives of others in order to better understand the changes which took place in their world.

The people that have given me their own story do so with the purpose of giving you the reader, a gift of them self. This gift offers encouragement, wisdom and the knowledge that change can bring greatness into your life.

With this new found knowledge, you can use it in your own life and let it will become a part of you. Hopefully you will allow these stories to give you the encouragement to change your own life. With that change you will have the ability to write your own 'story of change'.

For me, writing this book is about sharing experience that can have a positive effect upon other people. Everything we do in life has an impact on our lives and the lives of others.

A pebble dropped into the water, thousands of miles out in the vastness of an ocean creates a ripple. As this ripple moves out from the center they become waves. The winds will increase and carry them towards the shore.

Miles upon miles are travelled until the lapping of a wave begins against the shore. Waves can cause damage to shorelines and alter the landscape. They can also bring gifts of wonder to children playing in the sand. Shiny and beautiful sea shells to brighten ones day appear. A *message in a bottle* from some far off land can be found or imagined.

Your life is much like that pebble dropped into the ocean. It will have an effect upon your life and many others. The story you have, the experience gained by living; each will cause change in some one else's life.

So it is with great appreciation that I invite you as a guest to experience a new beginning, a new change. The stories which follow will give you hope and inspiration. Thank you for coming in and being a part of life.

Change Happens

*"Human beings, by changing the inner attitudes of their minds,
can change the outer aspects of their lives."*
William James

Many times we go through life believing that the path we are on was pre-chosen for us. All we can see is one narrow vision of a road that leads off in a direction that we simply are not happy with. So we try to adapt to the road, to the scenery and make the best of our travel.

We may pass an intersection along our way and wonder what lay down a path untaken. We stop at this crossroads and see something different on the horizon of the other path. Our interest is heightened but the *'map'* in our mind tells us to stay on our own path. So we continue down the same path, but with a growing sense that this isn't the correct one.

The feeling grows until one day you are standing at a *'crossroads of life'* and decide to make a change in your life. It is this change that people so often talk about. They are stories of change in attitude, personal revelation or change in direction that can impact others.

This impact upon other people with our stories is to describe what we did to change the course of our lives. There are those whom will say, *"no one would want to hear my story"* or *"it was such a small and insignificant thing."* These are precisely the stories that other people need to hear.

We find ourselves helping others with something as simple as our own story. And when you are unsure, then guess what...you may very well be standing at that crossroads looking down various paths at a new horizon.

Make a difference, make a change and let the story begin....

The Choice

A non-descript path crosses a grass field and leads up to the door of a lonely looking building. The path has obviously been used a number of times by those assembled inside. Worn and dirty, people have trudged along the path for quite some time.

The building is not much to speak of with its brick front and plain looking windows. One can tell that this building has been here for a number of years. It has the appearance of being old and tattered. Some might see potential in fixing it up while others would say it should be torn down.

A group of people are assembled inside. Those that come to this building daily will never tear it down and build a new one. Even with its worn look, they have a feeling of comfort and safety. Change does not fit into their lives.

When you enter the front door, you find a single large room filled with a vast assortment of chairs and tables that have the look of constant use. A cold tile floor with many cracked and missing pieces spreads throughout the room.

Your attention is barely drawn away by the artificial plants dotting the room. They are plastic reminders that life itself could not thrive in such a depressing place. Even the windows near the front door have a particular film of dirt covering them. If one were to look through them, the outside landscape appears blurred and unrecognizable.

There are old and outdated magazines scattered around on the tables which themselves are old and outdated. There are news, celebrity gossip, cooking and various sports magazines. Each are filled with events long past. Those that read them like the feeling of knowing what "*has happened*" much better then contemplating what "*might happen*." The future to them is too much to comprehend, but they still long for it.

As you make your way around, you notice the room is lit by fluorescent fixtures. This gives the room a cold feeling. The unnatural glow lights the walls which seem to have a floral or other odd pattern design.

When you look closer, you discover the walls are adorned with various pictures. Hundreds upon hundreds of pictures that could take a life time to look at each of them. None seem to have any relation to the other for they are dreams once dreamed, visions once envisioned and of hopes left scattered.

If you ask others, you will find that all of these were placed here by those gathered in the room. They are placed on these walls once given up, no longer to be pursued. Lives left on the walls in order to fade and be lost among the other lost dreams.

More people enter the room carrying their dreams in shiny boxes and crisp envelopes. Others move to the walls looking for their left behind dreams. Each has come into this room with anticipation of carrying forward their lives.

Now if you were to look directly through this building as you enter the front door, you would see a large oak door near the rear of the room.

It is near this rear door that the floor is not worn; the walls close by are untouched. It remains clearly different as many people never dare to come near it. The door is not particularly ornate but is enough to catch the eye of those entering.

Above the door is a sign which reads;
"Choose To Live Life - Choose Now"

When you choose to make a change, life begins to occur in ways that will forever transform you. Each of us faces this sign at some point in our lives. My life changed when I chose to finally walk through that door.

My life came to this same crossroads, facing a choice that would forever alter everything. Starting as a son born sixth of seven, in a time when being Catholic and having numerous children seemed normal.

This son would be a man one day facing a choice. I would be standing in that room, staring at a sign which is read by many others with stories of change. These stories arise from the ordinary to the most famous of people.

Each was faced with the need to change their lives and grow. The completion of my life and theirs has yet to be written, but we each made a choice.

These are our stories...

Choice At The Crossroads
Joseph Primm - USA

I always felt a certain familiarity to a Bible story regarding the *'Prodigal Son.'* The parable comes from Luke 15:11 and is a well known story told over and over. Was I the lost and wayward son that returned to the riches of my father? Or was I the son who remained behind?

Not exactly, but the lessons learned did return me to the riches of a full life. A life in which I became much more content and understanding of who I was and not someone that I thought others wanted me to be.

The story I tell is not earth shattering or filled with horror and chaos. No, it is a story of how I came to be standing in that room, looking at a sign above a door challenging me to make a choice.

Since I was one of the younger children in a large family, I learned quite a lot by watching my older siblings. The things one could do or not do and how certain actions were received by my parents. It allowed me to fit in as the *'good son.'*

My parents did a great job and as in any family, not everything was perfect. A large family can mean less material things but a learned appreciation for what one has. We worked hard and at times played hard.

It was during these formative years that I developed the 'good son' mentality. Do what was told of you, do it to your best and then do it even better. Being raised on a farm in eastern Nebraska allowed one to work hard as well. It was not always easy, but there are no complaints when one doesn't know anything different.

My father had a depression era view on many things. Save as much money as you can, reuse as much as you can and old stuff can be considered new if you are seeing it for the first time. Take old oak doors for instance, the old heavy ones that you rarely find these days.

There can be many uses for these doors if you put your mind to good use. On our small farm we raised hogs, the type that end up in the grocery store and on the dinner table. If you look at pictures of them in story books, they are cute and seemingly cuddly. To raise them is a different story and is a lot of work.

There are days that require you to divide them up, some for fattening, and others for market. The process can be quite challenging and it was the oak doors we used. An oak door with door knobs intact makes a great way to separate hogs. These doors are also quite heavy for a young boy that didn't have the physique of a football player.

We would find these doors at the old trash dumping location near our hometown. This dump was a ravine, back again during those times before much stricter regulations. That which we could not burn was taken to this dump.

Most times we returned with more then we took. This is the *new stuff* I referred to earlier. My father had a great *'eye'* for things that could be potentially used on our farm. He could spot an old oak door many yards away.

One such day he found one laying about half way down the ravine. All we had to do was climb down, attach a rope and pull it back up. I was the available son and was instructed to ensure that I tied up to it securely.

So down I went, doing as I was told, never wanting to disappoint. All the while I kept wondering if the whole trash pile would give way and slide further down the ravine. God was watching over me I am sure; no scrapes, no bruises and another prized oak door was ours.

Do not get this wrong, my father today has repeatedly wondered aloud what he could have been thinking.

The same could be said of our ability to tear down an old building, use the remains of it and build something new. Again, what is old to others is *new stuff* to us. Such as the old and unusable corn crib we had.

This time we would tear it down, saving all of the wood in order to build a '*new*' machine shed. The tin roof was carefully removed to be used for the sides of the new building. The roof boards would come in handy and the framing timbers were as good as gold.

The timbers would form the frame of the new building. So we had to be careful when pulling down the rafters of this old and reasonably unsafe corn crib. My father would be on the old tractor and I would climb up to attach a cable. With care my father would pull these down one by one.

A particular set of rafters were being troublesome and required a person to hold onto the adjoining rafters. This would prevent the whole structure from coming down. As I dutifully obeyed my father's instructions, I held on for dear life. His loud words of not to let go such that the structure might fall on him rang loud and clear.

"*On him!*" I thought, "*what about me coming down as well?*" But this is what a good son does. He obeys what he is told to do and never questions out loud. It was here that I first experienced the building near the crossroads in my mind.

What would I do, would it be different this time?

When high school drew to a close, college was what I felt could save me. I had a chance to leave the family fold and strike out on my own. Similar to what the *'prodigal son'* did, I left all that could have been mine for a different kind of life. College was the answer to my question, a place where I could be my own person.

I did all of those things a young person in college would do. I drank too much, played music too loud and didn't spend as much time as I should have on class work. But the overriding idea of the good son drew me into Student Body politics.

It was here that I became a member of the Student Council and worked my way up to Student Body President by the end of my first year. I had even been elected student representative to the state college governing board. Yes, I found myself falling back into doing what a *'good son'* does.

There were times I would rebel in my role of leadership. We held a *'sit-in'* of a faculty meeting room which was rarely used. Our student body activities were in need of space and it seemed perfectly logical to take over this area. I can say that our college president was not very happy with me.

I can also state now that it is never a good idea to upset the same faculty members that teach you in class and grade your progress. Their dislike of my actions did not go over very well on this small campus of 2000 students. It was time to get back in line and follow the dictates of doing what was expected of me.

But then the allure of freshmen girls came along in my second year. They were each a sight to behold and the yearnings of a young man were being pulled in a new direction. It was during this tempting time that I met one that would become my wife.

We fell in love and had plans to get married later the following year. Then life had a way of changing our plans. Our marriage would need to be moved up as a new child was on the way. The only choice and right choice was to quit school, get married, find a job and begin to raise a family.

And here I was, back in the '*good son*' mode doing what was the right and proper thing to do. I was going to show everyone that the choices I had made in life were the right ones. We went from one child, no money, no job and no place to live to so many bills and four children. I was doing the right thing, the good son was going to make good.

My focus in life has always been to try and be a good father, husband and support my family. It was a road taken and I saw no other choices to make. I continued to focus on working hard and taking advancement along the way. We moved from Lincoln, Nebraska to Aberdeen, South Dakota; onto Fargo, North Dakota (yes, that Fargo) and a big move to Atlanta, Georgia. All this time I was doing what was taught in following the rules, never understanding the real reasons why I should be doing all of this.

Upon our arrival in Atlanta though, there seemed to be a shift in what was happening in our lives. What seemed to work before didn't seem to work now. The kids were growing up and normal issues of raising children began to come up. The money never seemed to go far enough. I turned inward towards my job doing what I felt I was supposed to do.

As the bills continued to pile up, more work, more distance from my wife and increased drinking all around added to the disarray. Was this the expectation for my life? Was I going to struggle to the very end? I continued to tell myself that I was doing the right thing in being the good father and the good husband; in being the good son.

So I sunk back into doing the one thing I felt control over, which was work. I still had dreams and hopes for what our lives would be like. Growing old and seeing my sons all get great degrees, beautiful wives and wonderful jobs.

And then the dream of the building at the crossroads returned once again. It was a building with a door that would open onto the middle of a crossroads offering you options. I could see the gleaming ribbons of road going off in several directions.

In my dream, once a day people would enter a room in which they sit reading old magazines and talking in quiet tones of what could have been. Others move about the walls looking for their lost dreams. While some have entered the building for the first time with dreams and visions in hand. All of us were waiting for an appointed time. It is a time when a choice would need to be made.

Looking around at the four walls gives you the sense of how much yearning there is in this world. Each of the items left on the wall tells a story of something wanted and never gained. If only this person or that person had boldly stepped out in change. If only I would boldly step out in change.

Then it would happen, a large oak door opens and a person enters. A very handsome and well dressed person, almost seeming to float in an easy stride; unencumbered he draws the attention of all that are present. A brilliant glow shines through. All can see the wondrous landscape which lies beyond the open door. It is opportunity that each of us see.

In an easy and comforting tone, the person tells all assembled, *"the door is open for you to step through. Once outside, choose a path and let life unfold before you."*

Nothing more, no other enticements, just the promise that their lives will be different. I watch as a couple of people run forward with glee and expectation. They go through the open door, each carrying with them all that they want. Others hesitate and mumble to others around them. Unsure of what to do, they talk of what might happen or not happen by going through the door.

All know that to pass through that door means they can never return back through it. This old building, the old path back to their old lives isn't so bad. They stand around telling themselves that the *'time is not right.'*

For seven minutes the door remains open. Not a long time to make a decision one might say. But all of these people have been spending their whole life trying to decide. They came this far and have entered this building by the crossroads. The door is open and all it takes is a step of change.

The door then closes and the cold light of the room returns. Those remaining place their dreams and visions upon the wall, left there to be reclaimed tomorrow or forgotten by indecision. As they leave they can hear faint shouts of joy and happiness.

The noise comes from those that have passed through the oak door. From those that are on a new adventure down a new path, happy with whatever comes their way. What were their stories of change? They are stories of people that moved on from their circumstance, a defining moment we each eventually have.

Mission In Life
Paul – Peru

I guess if I had my way, change would be the few coins you received after you purchased your daily coffee. It's impersonal, none demanding and gives you the deceptive feeling in your pocket that you do have money. Unlike the real change we are talking about here, it tends to be quite the opposite.

Don't get me wrong, bear with me as I continue the ramble, change has been the most rewarding, life enhancing and memorable (in a good way) of experiences. But in most of life's experiences it involves a journey and an accompanying range of theme park ride emotions.

I am no psychologist but it seems that there are definite stages we tend to go through pre, mid and post change. The pre-phase usually involves a certain amount of dissatisfaction. You know the meaning of *"life/what's it all for"* type questions. I then search for a new meaning or direction.

Next comes the exciting part the planning phase, the dreams take shape, the possibilities, the impact. All well and good but next is the execution of those plans. I use the word execution because that is exactly how it feels.

Your head is on the block, with your only support being a cold block and of course the crowd watching. The swoosh of an axe comes along, but strangely you are still alive and breathing.

You get a heightened sense of the world and a new appreciation of what really matters replaces those last meal preoccupations. But you are up and stumbling and it's awesome. Your gait becomes more stable and confidence begins to leak into your thoughts. At this point I have to acknowledge other factors other than myself for the new world experience.

Why at this point? Well because when you're in the dark, your thoughts do not naturally turn to warm and fuzzy feelings about your creator, your family and friends. Of course they were there, they are just as nervous as you are about your future. A nervous God? Well it makes for a good story. It is probably time to contextualize the story.

After ten years as an assistant pastor of a church, I moved to the South American country of Peru. I started my own non-profit organization and began helping others in need. Wow, that was so easy to write; a few keystrokes that contain a major life reroute.

Leaving my old life proved to be a tough assignment. When D-Day arrived I needed some coaxing. There were good friends of mine that gently pried me out of my familiar world.

Those birthing pains continued as I arrived in Lima, Peru on a cold and clammy July night. You must remember that it would be the middle of winter in the southern hemisphere.

I was dropped off at an address that could best be described, not wanting to offend anyone, as very basic. A better description is to say that a good day was just to have water. An even better day was to have hot water.

I lived in a world of car alarms, burglar alarms and continual remodeling; the source of which I could never locate. The apartment was in an ideal location from where I could walk most anywhere. There were excellent restaurants nearby, however some days it felt like I was actually living in the kitchens of these culinary establishments.

Inexplicable it seemed that the smoke and fumes vented into my apartment. A burning, acrid sensation greeted my eyes and nose whenever I flung open the door. Retreating to the bedroom proved of no respite. It was there as well!

Diving into bed to escape turned into a lesson of balance and coordination the likes of a gymnast would be proud. The base of my bed was smaller than the mattress upon which it rested. It became like a one man seesaw ride. Remember those ancient apparatus you used to find in the local park before fear of litigation made them disappear.

A turn one way too far would result in me and my mattress hitting the floor. A quick flip back usually took care of the situation and I would be steadied enough to fall asleep or inhale a lungful of the sweet fragrance of the nightly fried specials from next door.

I would awake at a very early hour each day. Just outside my window and I tell no lies, was completely covered in a black mixture of Lima dirt and restaurant grease. A Pavarotti perched pigeon would begin his morning rehearsals.

The airplane earplugs I picked up on the flight down proved to be no match for this bird. His throat and lungs belted out 'cooee' in several octaves for a good hour.

Getting out of bed was easy; remember it was a trick bed. I would stumble to the bathroom to see if today it was going to be water, hot water or a no water day.

Did I mention the termites which had a colony in the bathroom cabinets? Every morning I would clean away several piles of digested wood excrement which had been expertly arranged in cone shaped patterns.

My opportunity to change the world came unexpectedly and rather shockingly. It all began in the local supermarket and it was in the chocolate aisle to be precise. Not that I was lingering, looking longingly at the vast array of chocolate products.

I was just passing by when I thought I heard a freight train in the fruit and vegetable section, somewhere near aisle 2.

I thought it was one of those marketing gimmicks, much like the thunder and rain simulators that mist the vegetables or the hidden speakers that place mooing cows behind the dairy fridges in U.S. grocery stores.

No, it was an earthquake and around a 7.0 to be precise. Having never experienced one before I was, shall I say scared. While it was happening I was like *"Umm..what is this!! What do I do!!"*

All was well until the screams and stampede interrupted what was until then an enjoyable experience. The chocolates which I had been not looking at started to bounce off the shelves; all I could see was chocolate.

I'm not sure if the alarms woke me out of my bliss or the shrieks of sprinting middle aged women but instinct took over and I bolted like an Olympic runner from the store.

Next I experienced what I would call the ripple effect and in no sense did it have to do with economics. The ground of the parking lot was rippling, just like the surface of a lake after you throw in a rock.

Did change come my way? It did in ways that I had not been able to foresee. A year later and my mission work have created an impact in the lives of so many.

There are children going to school where once they didn't have supplies to study. There are children and adults with better health due to better medical care. There are some of the first children going to college where once they could not.

Much more can and will be written, but change came my way and changed me forever.

~~~~~~

Paul O'Connell is founder of the non-profit organization
Open Road Missions - www.openroadmissions.com -

~~~~~~

Letting Go Of Guilt
Pam – USA

My life is like so many others in that you find your self carrying the weight of so many issues. We gather issues dealing with trust, love, guilt or so many others. It becomes overwhelming such that life becomes an obstacle unto itself.

After my sister died, I soon learned that if you love someone, you always feel guilt after their death. You allow the guilt to rise in you for not doing more, saying more, or just being there.

The guilt becomes a chain to moving on with life. Many times the guilt felt so tight around my body, so much that I could not breathe. So many times I felt that '*if only*' I had done this or that. '*If only*' the days could be repeated, so much more I would have done for her.

Just saying and feeling "*I feel guilty*" is an excuse to feel pity for your self. It does not help the person whom is now gone and it certainly does not help you to grow and learn.

My change came when I learned that you have to review the guilt and learn from them or throw them away. The guilt that you feel may not be valid, but sometimes it's hard to be objective of your own faults.

Just learn from the experience and do not allow it to happen again. I changed the view of guilt in my life. You can change your view of guilt in your life as well. Learn and grow from it.

Back From Under
Kristien – USA

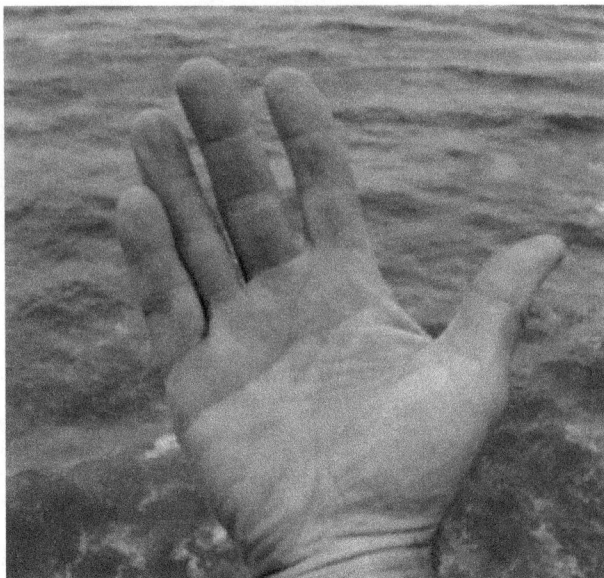

Well, I guess you could say that my story started years ago. I grew up in a loving home. We didn't really like to associate a "*title*" to our Christianity, but it could be described best as non-denominational or Pentecostal.

I attended a private school my whole life. It had great academics, but there was one problem that would follow me my whole life. This school was religious and when I say religious, I mean CRAZY religious.

They claimed to be non-denominational, and had a good mix of denominations, but the owners and many of the teachers were all extremely legalistic.

This is where most of my issues began to grow. I grew up (from K-5, so I was around 5-6 yrs old when I started attending this school) listening to men (and an occasional woman [they didn't believe women should be pastors]) tell us how everything is wrong and one should live a strict rigid lifestyle.

When I returned home, my parents would teach us the opposite. They would teach us freedom and acceptance in God. Despite their extreme religiousness, I decided to accept Jesus Christ as my savior.

So naturally I grew up confused. Adolescence hit and my life really got crazy. Like every child-becoming-a-man does, I decided to rebel against everything that I had been taught from both the school and my parents.

I decided that God wasn't helping me out enough. I guess you could call me a *"lukewarm"* Christian. I talked the talk when I was around Christians, but when it came to walking the walk, I was not there.

I was about 12 yrs old when I started smoking cigarettes. The following year I started drinking at friends houses, and by the time I was 14 I was smoking pot as well.

In 1996 my family started attending a church in the Atlanta area called '*Christian City Church*.' It was there I began to learn about true Christianity and being set free from religion. Obviously this didn't hit home until much later, but it turned out to be crucial in the greatest change my life would ever see.

On October 15, 1996 my father was killed in a car accident. I was only 15 years old at the time. To a troubled youth, such as I was, this was devastating; but it didn't stop there.

There was a kid in one of the younger grades that I looked at as my protégé. Later that year, he hung himself. The cops ruled it as an accidental death, that he was trying to scare his mom and the joke turned out badly, but we never really new.

The following years dealt even more death to me and my younger brother. Two of his friends died tragically. The first was hit by a car and died in his brother's arms, while the second, drug induced, plummeted off of a cliff in a rock quarry, hit his head on a rock and drown.

We were all very close. The excruciating pain of loss drove me to find an alternative to fill the void that I had in my soul. I tried to hold on to church, believing that there was a reason for all of this, but all I could muster was a crude façade. I didn't really know who God was and what it meant to be a true follower of Christ.

By the time I was 16, I was drugged out of my mind and suicidal. At this point in my life, '*ecstasy*' was my drug of choice: ecstasy, acid, and special K (ketamine, a cat tranquilizer).

Six weeks before graduation, in 1999, I was expelled from the school I was attending. Apparently my past caught up with me. You can fool around in school for only so long. I had to finish at a public high school. We had moved a year earlier, closer to the church we were attending.

Later that year I was arrested for a DUI. Lucky for me the sheriff never checked for drugs. He only gave me a sobriety test, which I miserably failed. I got a lawyer and had it dropped to reckless driving. Even so, I still had defensive driving and DUI School to do, community service, an MRT (moral recognition therapy) class, and probation.

My time on probation allowed me to clean my system from all of the drug use. I quit using ecstasy, acid, and special k. I tried to end my suffering when exactly 3 months to the day that I quit ecstasy by trying to overdose on OTC drugs.

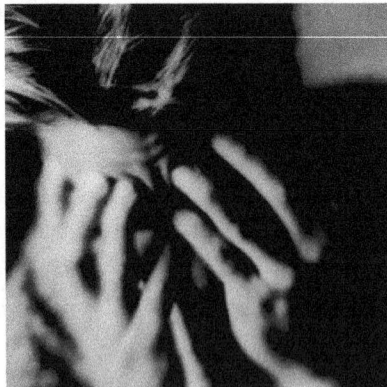

God had different plans for obviously I didn't die, but boy did I have one hell of a stomach ache later. I stopped smoking pot for a while, but never quit drinking. Time passed and things just got worse. I flunked out of college, lost a few jobs, and found my way to selling cocaine. At the time, this was my new drug of choice. I started just snorting and ended up using needles intravenously.

I had left church and shunned anyone that went or that tried to connect to me. I was hurt by friends and leaders in the church by the way they had treated my family. The hypocrisy of people fueled my anger even more. I tried many different religions and spiritualities, including ancient Egyptian mythology, to find the truth about life. I was hurting, angry, depressed, and feeling alone and isolated.

Through my own sheer will I had quit smoking cigarettes, but I drank even more. I finally hit bottom after a failed drug deal. Lives were hanging on a thread. I had an epiphany that it was time to quit. This was the third time in my life that I contemplated suicide. I decided to quit using cocaine.

My life had spiraled out of control and thought I had reached the depth of depravity that I could go no further. I was wrong. Drinking became my newest obsession. Every day and every night we drank. We drank until we would pass out, then get up and drink some more. I treated everyone around my like they were nothing. I hated everything and everyone. In my mind God did this to me.

You see, I knew there was a God. I knew the Judeo-Christian God existed. I had been an atheist to a Satanist. I knew that God was there, I just hated Him. I despised Him for what my life had become. I hated anyone that tried to help, including family. I just wanted to watch the world die, like me. One night, at my mother's home, my brother was having a party. Naturally we were drunk as can be. I had started that morning with my brother.

My mother was not amused by the party and started trying to talk some sense into a few of us. It escalated to an argument and I lost my mind. I pulled a knife on my own mother. I started screaming while cutting myself and pointing the knife at her. Luckily my oldest brother was there to beat me down and take the knife away.

I can still remember to this day the way I felt the next morning. I called my mom and apologized. We talked it through a bit and we got a number for a psychiatrist from our pastor. This was one of the best things I could have done in my life.

I still hated God at this point in time. I found that a lot of confusion was helping to fuel my anger. The vast majority of this confusion was from my time at the private school. Because of my alcoholism, I quit drinking for a year and a half to get things under control. During this time I started smoking a lot more weed than I ever did. In a way it helped to mellow out my crazy behavior.

Finally, a woman who had stood by me through most of my life came to live with me for a second time as a friend. I had already started going back to church every now and then. I had begun to forgive those people that had wronged me and asked forgiveness from those that I had wronged.

This friend, this woman pushed me to go to church more with her, and because of her I began to see God and the Christian faith in a new light. One night lying in bed, I prayed without yelling and screaming blasphemies at God.

I asked that if this woman was the right one for me, to soften my heart so that I could love her. In that instant I felt warmth I had never felt spread from my chest throughout my body.

From that moment on I realized that God had never left me. That he still cared after everything I'd done. A few months later I participated in a program at my church which further changed my life.

My life would never be the same. God touched me more than I had ever felt. I finally knew what freedom and redemption were. All those early years of being taught by my parents and the church hit home. For the first time in many years I felt loved and a part of something special. I eventually quit smoking pot and took charge of my life.

I received two promotions within a year of each other, certified myself in networking and started a new life with my friend. We have been married a year now and have a beautiful baby boy named after my father.

God has blessed me more than I can ever repay. I have made many changes in my life, but believing in God and having the faith to trust His will and let Him lead, has been the greatest change I have ever made.

The Important One
Rhubarb – USA

On February 29, 2008 a meeting was called in a conference room. No one knew of what would transpire. We were given envelopes with our severance package and told that due to economic cut backs most of the full time broadcaster's jobs were eliminated. I was fired? How could this happen to me?

Wasn't I a winner of numerous awards and accolades including being a member of the elite Country Music Disc Jockey Hall of Fame without a job for the first time in my life?

I didn't let those thoughts take root. I looked at it as an opportunity to do something that truly contributes to the lives of others that I had wanted to do for a long time. Teaching was something I had thought about for a long time. I went to graduate school at Shorter College and worked hard to get a 4.0 grade point average with the dream of being a teacher at the college level.

Approximately 72 hours after being fired my phone rang and on the other end was Dr. Dan Papp, President of Kennesaw State University. He wanted me on his team.

I can't tell you how thrilled I was after working 36 years in a culture with few pats on the back. I knew what my destiny would be. It was the turning point in my life that has given me a chance to work in an arena that is so rewarding. Seeing a student's face light up when you make a point is something I never had in radio broadcasting.

Do I miss radio? I miss the listeners and the people who were so kind and loyal to me all those years. Do I miss getting up at 3:45 a.m.? I can tell you, not at all.

Would I ever do radio again? I am having too much fun working in a field that truly can shape the lives of individuals. Next to the birth of my children, getting fired was the best thing that has ever happened to me.

I discovered who my true friends are upon getting handed the door. Do I look back? No, I am too busy forging ahead.

~~~~~~

Rhubarb Jones is a former Atlanta radio personality and now a distinguished lecturer and Director of Special Projects in University Development at Kennesaw State University.

~~~~~~

Standing At Attention
Dave – USA

I was whiling away my late teens/early 20s in a mountain town where no one went anywhere, as a fry cook. We thought we were pretty cool, we worked hard and made what we thought was good money but really, we were going nowhere.

We were also drinking and smoking stuff we should not have been; spending all of our cash on partying and driving around California. There was the doping and even more partying.

As far as leaving home, I was not ready for the real world after 7 years in a tiny village. But I knew I had to do something, so I moved off to the city, crashed with a friend for a while and started looking for a place to live and a job.

This was in San Diego where there are a lot of distractions and finding a place to live is difficult - not a cheap place anyway. Some of my prospective roommates were downright creepy.

Jobs didn't look so attractive either; all of my experience was in restaurants. But I finally got some good prospects lined up for a day's travels, both job interviews and places to stay. I went out to start my car and – nothing, it would not start.

I never did find out what was wrong with the car - took it in, they checked it out, found nothing and it never did that again. But it screwed up my appointments all right.

And while it was in the shop I wandered over to the Army recruitment office and, as they say, the rest is history. I signed up, went off to Ft. Benning and became an infantryman. After four years there, the regular world was just going to be too easy.

One of Milt's Signs
John - USA

I graduated high school in a small rural eastern Nebraska town with very little knowledge of the "*world*" and could not wait to escape the confines of what I viewed as an oppressive environment.

I believe in those days that I had a failure complex and felt that everybody and everything in life was slanted against me. I was constantly fighting the system and trying to prove I was right and all else wrong.

That in itself was bad enough, but it was somewhat harmless except for people's perception of me, which at that age is not much of a concern. What happened after high school was personally disastrous to my life and many around me for too many years.

I entered the Army at age eighteen and left it at twenty-one, a much changed person, a change that left many relationships with friends and family in ruins. I could cover all the gory details and recount the particulars, but I prefer to just say I was a miserable failure for quite a few years and blamed everyone around me for my troubles.

I had reached a point where most of the people in my life either disassociated themselves from me, or hoped I would leave them alone. I can't tell you how many actually put up with me and helped me limp along while trying to find my way to a better life. During that period, I never recognized what I was like or the efforts it took for people to tolerate me.

To make a long story even longer, seven years after graduation I was about one to two inches from the bottom of the barrel. I was penniless, close to homeless and not seeing any real chances of improving the situation.

I was looking for a job anywhere with no luck, moving from bit work to hand outs for helping on daily labor, when I walked by a clothing store with a help wanted sign in the window.

There I was, fully confident that the outcome of me going in and applying would be the typical '*thanks but no thanks*'. I turned to walk away when a gentleman smoking a cigarette in a little cigarette holder asked if I was looking at the help wanted sign.

I replied that I was but knew I probably couldn't get that kind of job. That's when the gentleman who was Milt Harm, manager of the store introduced himself and invited me in to "*just talk*".

Well, though I didn't know it at the time, this man was my savior. He sat me down and asked about me about myself. Well let me tell you that was a tough conversation,

I tried to highlight only the positive experiences and jobs but found that on paper, it would resemble Swiss cheese. Old Milt was pretty wise and must have figured me out right away. He asked if I would like a temporary job and I accepted.

Life working for Milt ended up being very similar to life with my own father. If I didn't know better, I could have sworn he would call my father every now and then to see what he could make me do next.

Milt worked me twelve hours a day and along the way taught me the value of hard work, respect for others, professionalism, respect for myself, responsibility, honesty, and a few other characteristics that are important in life.

I didn't have time to party anymore, he rented me an apartment above the store and that helped to semi-domesticate me, and gave me a new found desire to make others happy.

That job, that 'Man' helped my life take an immediate turn and I remember him as a surrogate father to this day. I do want to mention that much of the things Milt did to me and for me was close to exactly what my father tried to teach us all in our youth, I just wasn't listening at the time.

I'm listening now and life has changed for the better.

I'm Pregnant
Anonymous - USA

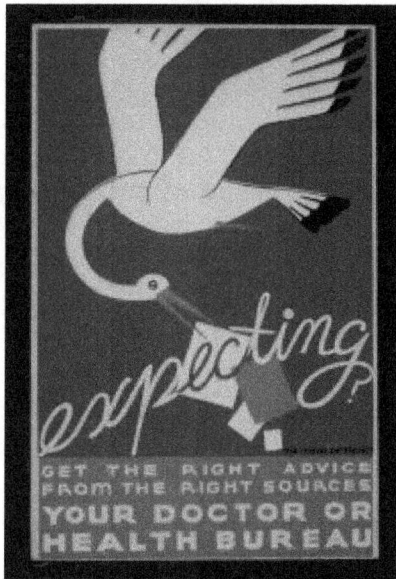

expecting?

GET THE RIGHT ADVICE FROM THE RIGHT SOURCES YOUR DOCTOR OR HEALTH BUREAU

"I'm pregnant," were the first words I heard on the phone that evening. Here I am, seventeen years old and in my senior year of high school. I went outside to where my father and I had been doing some work.

He knew something was wrong. I said I needed to see her as soon as I could. I think he knew what was wrong. We met that evening, talked, cried, hugged and we knew what had to be done.

Such a thing in our community was almost unheard of. The stares, jokes and rumors were very hard but we knew what had to be done. We knew, although our church and state law would not allow this to happen in our state.

Our parents were shocked and saddened. School was in the future for both of us but now our lives would be forever changed.

Our parents, families and true friends were very supportive by our decision and we went ahead with it. This story could have ended a number of different ways, so you could draw your own conclusions.

Our lives have changed forever, changed with the support of our families and friends. Thirty five years of marriage, children and now grandchildren are the result of our lives having been changed forever.

This may or may not be the decision you thought we made but it was the ONLY option we considered. This was not our only life changing experience but it is our most precious. Thank you to all who have stood by us from the very first.

Cycle Of My Life
Tim - USA

The day was August 2, 2008. It was a typical hot humid day in Covington, Georgia at the start of what should end as a 100 mile ride through eight towns and five counties.

Cyclists train diligently for the challenge of the century ride and it has become a right of passage from recreational rider to enthusiast cyclist for most who attempt it.

The ride is not really a race but a test of endurance, stamina, mental toughness and pain tolerance. It requires a death grip on the cyclist true ability and the discipline to ride within that ability for over six hours.

Over 900 cyclists would leave the starting line with some of them only targeting to finish a 30, 50 or 80 mile course. All leave together and all striving to finish at their target finish and take their cycling to the next level.

A few people show up out of shape and ride 100 miles in a day. Some will have trained for months and sometimes all year for this event. Everyone who sets out on this journey has a story.

For me it all began in May of 2007 when I went on my first church '*C3 Journey*' event. I had been in the church for 8 years and this event had been going on for most of the time.

Since I had a military background and having gone through some of the most grueling training Army Rangers could dish out, I didn't think a journey was for me.

I was older now, married and about fifty pounds heavier than when I was in my prime. But at the encouragement of the event leadership and a nod from my wife, I reluctantly signed up.

The first day of the journey I was passive aggressive. You know the move; you act like you are into it when all the time you hate every minute. You keep telling yourself how stupid all this is and how it is not for you and you can't wait until it's over and you can say it was all a bunch of hooey.

Well, that was me only I didn't expect the gracious intervention of the Holy Spirit to tap me on the shoulder and get my attention about my inner turmoil.

You see, I wasn't fighting against the '*Journey*', I was holding up the wall that was separating me from having to face the issues that God wanted to address in my life.

There were many issues that were brought to the surface during the three day journey to the center of the man. But the one that was on the top of the list was my physical health.

Sure sounds trivial doesn't it?

What does your health have to do with your eternity and for that matter the eternal plan that God has for you in building His Kingdom? I don't have all of the answers, but I have found that God works in an Arena.

Meaning, he finds an area of my life that he can shine His light on and it becomes the context for faith and practice. That arena becomes the Coliseum for my battles and the occasion for God to show me my weakness and demonstrate His strength.

I may not want to go into that arena. I may trivialize or marginalize it, blame others that I shouldn't have to fight in it, but in the end it is MY arena. For some it may be finances, marriage, children, sickness, church, school etc. What ever it is, that Arena is where God is and it is where I have found that my growth in God takes place.

The '*beast of burden*' for me had become my poor fitness and the lifestyle that had led to it. On the '*Journey*', each of us wrote out our own burden on the large and heavy log we called the '*BEAST*'. We then lifted that beast and tossed it to the ground, which is when the Coliseum was built for me. From that point forward I would be the gladiator fighting what ever came into that arena. And the clanging sound of my journey dog tags would be the reminder that the strength of my brothers was behind me.

I would like to say that after the journey I started an exercise program, started eating healthy and in just a few months I was back on track to living a healthy happy life.

That was just not the case. I got my hind end beat down with diet programs; exercise video's I hated; knee soreness from running and walking; discouragement and weight gain-weight loss yo-yo.

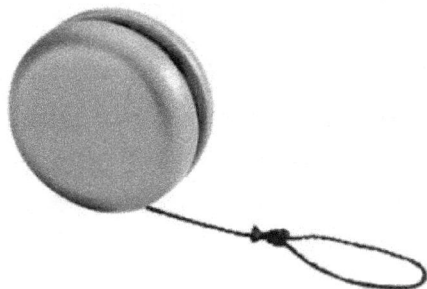

You name it; I was mopping the floor with my defeat. But still I knew that this was an area that God was in and I had to be diligent to let Him guide and empower me into victory while growing closer to Him in the process.

In a last ditch effort to do something I jumped on my Wal-Mart mountain bike that had only been ridden in the neighborhood with my daughter and set out to see if biking would be the thing.

I rode from my house to a near-by town which is about 3 miles and back and thought, *"This is something I could get into"*. I knew some of the guys in the church were cyclists and so inquired with them about riding. Each of them encouraged me and pointed me in the right direction. So I purchased a second hand road bike and started riding.

Soon a C3 Cycling Team had formed to meet for rides once a week and after grueling rides at paces that left me breathless with legs of jelly, I would listen to the stories of the triathlons and century rides along with all the bike gear tech talk and it encouraged me to keep improving.

I set up a personal plan and schedule for riding, worked out the family logistics of taking the time out, and kept a journal of my progress. I was finally starting to win in this arena and things were looking better.

I was losing weight at a healthy pace, I was eating right and now my exercise was fun and challenging and as a bonus, I got to do it with cool C3 guys.

All was going well at a nice pace until someone mentioned a century ride in August. It was only two months away and to that point the longest I had ever ridden was 35 miles. But hey I have two months to train.

I talked with the guys about training and researched what it takes and although it was a stretch, I signed up and started my training. Four-hundred fifty miles later and 30 pounds lighter than my journey weight, with a good understanding of; my max heart rate, average heart rate, sustainable effort, most efficient cadence and my personal hydration requirements, I arrived at the ride of the century.

The goal for the C3 Team was to stay together and work together to finish strong at the end. Well that plan sort of unraveled at the start line with nine-hundred other cyclists all jockeying for position and pace. Some how I was ahead of most of the guys on the team at the beginning and at the pace I was going I thought they would catch me at any minute.

They finally did catch me about eight miles in and I rode with them to the first stop at mile twenty-five. Everyone looked strong there. The adrenaline was pumping, we were working together as a team and everything was firing just right.

Team cycling is an amazing thing. At my level now I can maintain an average of about 16.5 miles an hour for about 30 to 50 miles. With a team I can average about two miles an hour faster if I am rotating off the front and resting up in the back.

Most of the effort is made at the front of a group as they take the head wind and break it for the guys behind and the guys behind can more easily keep the pace with less effort than the guys at the front.

The problem with this is that when you are in the group you may not be operating within your own abilities and working harder than you can sustain for the distance in order to stay with the group. Add in head wind, inclines and short periods of catching up and you have a recipe for disaster.

Our team stuck together for about another five miles and I kept looking at my heart rate and my pace and I was not seeing the finish line in my future. I dialed it back and nearly choked on my pride as team after team whizzed by me. Until finally I had caught my wind again and along came a group of riders I could keep pace with.

They pulled me in to the next rest stop at about 44 miles where I was coming in and the leaders of my team were pulling out. I quickly fueled and hydrated and off I went. I caught up with two of my team members who had hammered on ahead and they were noticeably taxed and fading fast.

In true team form we quickly found a pace we could all work together on and caught our collective breath before coming to the next break. The three of us pulled out together and rode the longest, straightest, upwind road I have ever been on.

Although we were working together, the heat and upwind effort was proving to show its wear on my team mates. I was entering a distance that I had never done before but I was doing it at a pace and effort that was well within my capacity so I was used but not used up. We pulled into the refueling stop at mile 65 and as before the leaders of the team were pulling out as we were pulling in.

At the stop there were guys laid out all over the place. Weary cyclists were stretching out cramped legs, dousing their heads with water and force feeding themselves with bananas. I had been eating and drinking every ten minutes so all I needed was to refuel my on board supply and top off the Gatorade.

The other two guys and one other from the lead out had to take an extended rest and rehydration break. I hung with them trying to encourage them to keep going but it was obvious they needed to cool the engine. Mean while I was concerned if I stayed too long I might cool and possibly cramp, so I pushed on.

The next 22 miles were some of the most testing of the day. I was alone for most of this leg of the ride. The climbs seemed steeper, the head wind stronger and the scenery-well it was plowed fields. I ate going up hill to take my mind off of the effort and drank going down hill to refresh.

And then came along a guy who was obviously stronger than I but seemed to be content to ride together and chat at my pace as we took turns taking the front and talking about club rides. He asked if I was in the military to which I said yes but wondered why he asked. It was then that I realized that I had my journey dog tags on and they were dangling from my neck.

It wasn't anything miraculous like a burning bush or the speed to out run the king's chariot but just then some how I felt strong knowing this was a continuation of the journey and the strength of many was also my strength.

We came up on my team leaders on the side of the road fixing a flat. Our two strongest cyclists had been tapped of most of their strength from the blistering pace set by others, who we learned were only doing 50 miles of the ride, and the demoralizing affects of the third tire flat. I joined them for the last mile or so to the next stop at 78 miles in. The team was all together at this stop. The guys who had been behind me had decided to call it a day. One of our guys who rode on an injured ankle for 40 miles rode back the other 40 miles after repairing a broken chain. We got a new tire to fix the flat problem and the last remaining three guys on the team set out to finish.

The plan was to stick together and go at a moderate pace to the finish. One of the guys was cramping up bad and I hung back with him for several miles hoping that the cramps might work themselves out but he finally sent me on ahead and had to pull over to try and stretch them out.

The next 12 miles would be the most beautiful and easiest miles of the ride. The route took us though gorgeous shaded roads in front of large estates and beautiful lakes. Another part would be a prairie like scenery with a blessed tail wind.

Nothing revives the soul like a tail wind. You ride faster and feel lighter than ever. I finished that leg of the ride just looking ahead at short goals. At this point man and machine had become just machine. There was the heart rate gauge and the pace and the hydration and the fuel and the effort and the next rider just off in the distance.

One by one I caught and passed five riders before the next stop. At this point in the race there was no one I could see riding together. No teams, just individual efforts against the elements.

The final stop was at 90 miles and it is now the hottest part of the day. There were not a lot of people at this stop, not much talking, mostly grunts and sighs as bags of ice were dropped down the back of the shirt.

Our strongest leader was there but I didn't know where. I saw his bike and looked for him while filling up but couldn't find him. I had to pedal on toward the end of the journey.

Just shortly after pulling out of the break area the guy who had ridden with me earlier pulled up with one other guy and we started working together toward the finish. Lucky for me both guys were much bigger than me which means they blocked more wind. I would pull up the hills and they would ride front on the flats. At this point fueling and hydrating had become almost automatic. I emptied my first bottle in 20 minutes and the ice pack on my back broke at about mile 95.

By the end I was feeling euphoric. Would I sprint ahead of these guys at the end? Would there be throngs of people cheering as we finished?

I sped up slightly to be just a wheel ahead of the guy next to me. As I looked ahead there was no throng of people, only a line that we rolled across rather uneventfully. No sprint to the finish, no photo, just a number on the pavement that will be etched in memory: **100 miles.** It was the finish line.

I can't describe the feeling after that. The whole ride I was doing my best not to blow up physically or mentally. I was in territory I had never been in before and there were so many unknowns. Would I cramp up? Would I get heat exhaustion or nausea? Would I hit my limit before I hit the finish?

But now I had finished and I didn't injure myself. What a relief and what a ride. No other word can describe it except Ooh-Raa!

The journey this far for me has been about fitness but has translated to a life lesson that is shaping my world. God intends for me to take on life much like he has taught me to take on the arena of my physical fitness.

- Accepting the *"Arena"* that God want to use in my life
- Looking to Him and my brothers for guidance.
- Looking to Him and my brothers for encouragement.
- Planning wisely to succeed.
- Diligent in execution
- Finding the right *"weapons"* to win the fight.
- Training to grow stronger and increase endurance
- Living life within my limits
- Growing closer to God within the challenge.

I have now hit a mile stone or a 100 mile stone! But this is not the end. It's not about the miles or the weight or even about my fitness level.

For me it is about letting God get into any and every area of my life. There will be other challenges and other arenas that God will put his finger on. He will want to improve some area by His direction and other areas because of the circumstances of my choices, the choices of others or just life happenings.

There will be times I miss the mark and times when it takes way too long to see any success. Yet I know that the One who has called me is faithful and in this I am confident even if I am not confident in anything else.

Whatever your *"Coliseum"* may be I pray that you will find the strength of God, the partnership of the men and women in your life and the courage to make it *"The Story of the Century"*.

Power of the Right Coach
Cleopatra Bell – USA

Oprah Winfrey has Maya Angelou, Diana Ross has Berry Gordy Jr., Mariah Carey had Tommy Mottola, and Cleopatra Bell has Coach Kristi Lucariello.

I remember praying to God and writing it out as a goal, *"I want a coach to help me reach my personal and professional goals."* At that time I didn't have the money to pay a coach, some coaching fees start at $150.00 hour, however I had a strong desire to work with one. I had enough faith in God and my angels of prosperity that they would work it out!

Wow! Surprise! God has a way of answering your prayers bigger and better than you can imagine. I remember hearing about Coach Kristi Lucariello, from Bonnie Ross-Parker, the author of *Walk In My Boots-The Joy of Connecting.*

Kristi was starting a Women's Entrepreneur Success Group lovingly known as WE Success. She created this group as a way for her to give back.

She asked for a love offering of five to ten dollars; if you weren't able to give, that was fine, because no one was monitoring. The money we collected was given back to us, if we wanted a scholarship to participate in an event.

The group met every week for about two years with ten to twenty women attending. This group was an opportunity to share our dreams, resources and what was going on within each of us.

It also gave me the biggest opportunity to expose my limited thinking and my self-defeating belief system. Until that moment, I wasn't aware that I had any.

Kristi would open up with our WE Success Prayer, and we would share. Here is an example of my sharing: "*Hi, my name is Cleopatra Bell. I am a screenwriter, and I have branded myself as the feel good writer with a twist of spirituality. My passion is to write inspirational scripts for film, television, and the Internet that will impact the lives of people in a positive and empowering way.*" Come on now, be honest, doesn't that sound rich?

With my Toastmaster International experience, I know how to let it roll off my tongue with smoothness. Coach Mariette Durack Edwards, and Kristi helped me tweak my brand.

There was just one problem: I had a lot of duality in my belief system which I'll discuss later and was too attached to how it would happen, which prevented it from coming true. I've written numerous scripts: *Souls Connecting, In A Year, I'll Be Married*, and *The Secret to Life* are just a few.

I've taken many screenwriting and writing classes. I've been featured in magazines. I've had several subscriptions to many screenwriting and writing magazines, won honorable mention in a screenwriting contest, and served on the board of Women in Film Atlanta.

I remember sending Kristi an article from Essence magazine that detailed the struggle of being black and female in Hollywood. She brought the article to the group. I was so embarrassed that I could have died, but I held back my tears that day.

Kristi verbalized my biggest fear, since I was black and female I wouldn't have an opportunity in Hollywood. If I did, I would have to fight for it. This is one of the things I feared. I realized that Kristi and I had two different legacies: she is white and I am black.

One thing I learned, the memories of your ancestors are lodged in your genes. I wonder how many millions of black people are operating from this paradigm and have chosen to give up completely. Rutha Zackery once told me, *"Many times you may have opposition; however, you're still limitless."*

I accept that I am responsible for creating my success. I have even read in certain inspirational books to look for challenges; however, most people don't want them.

Many people will take the path of least resistance or self-medicate with drugs and alcohol. Being black and living the 'black' experience is unique in many ways; for example, my race has been programmed to believe in limitations and expect hardships because of our race.

Of course, the group encouraged me that I could make it. My WE Success Sister Sandra Gardner, CEO of Gardner Unlimited, gave me a copy of Time magazine featuring successful black women.

However, that wasn't enough, because deep down inside, I still felt even though they had achieved success, that wasn't my story. I recognized inside myself that I am an individual part of a culture, however we are on this journey of life and people evolve at different rates.

Kristi helped me when she shared these words, *"Once you clear this block it will help you, your family, and your community."* She stressed that what I focus on expands in my life--there are plenty of writing opportunities for me--that should be my focus. I thank her for her opinion.

Since we are talking about Hollywood, one of the beliefs is, *"It's not what you know but who you know."* I felt like I wasn't well connected, since I wasn't the daughter of Michael Eisner, CEO of the Walt Disney Corporation.

Kristi stressed over and over again, we are connected to *"THE SOURCE"* (God), and we must trust and have faith in that source to give us our heart's desires. Always focus on adding positive feelings and emotions to what we want to create.

Never give any energy or emotions to what we don't want to create in our lives. I have always gone to church. The truth is, I have intellectually known spiritual truths, but I didn't internalize them. I learned that from Coach Elyse Hope Killoran; Coach Kristi presented her materials to the group, and they were quite helpful in releasing duality in my thinking.

Elyse Hope Killoran turned me on to my current life coach Kathy Atkinson. Her coaching deals with how to flow your energy using Emotional Freedom Techniques to raise your vibration in creating your heart's desire.

Kathy has been able to assist me in releasing self-defeating beliefs and patterns by using Emotional Freedom Techniques. I have always had clarity about what I wanted out of my life, but I realized I spent more time focusing on the size of the gap between where I am and where I want to go.

I prayed and asked God to help me realize that God is the source of my supply, not a person, place, or condition. Kristi stressed again that there are several agents out there looking for me.

My WE Success Sister Donya Robinson, one of the founders of the *Sharing Center For Women* turned me to the law of detachment. The law of detachment means you have clarity of the goal/desire but, you don't outline how it should happen.

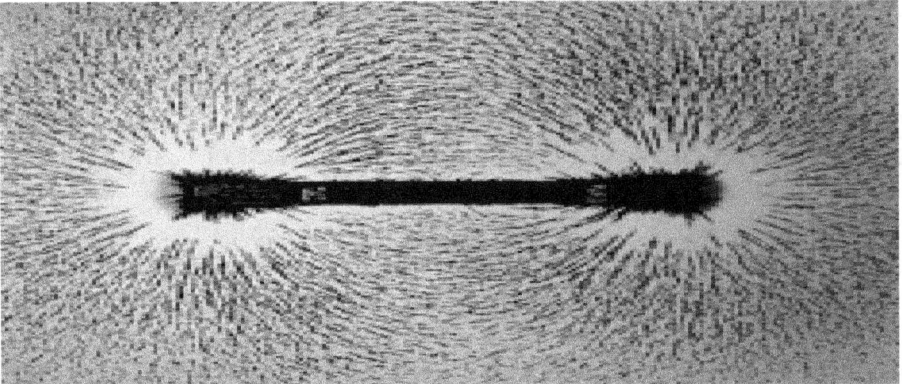

One of the best resources Kristi turned the group on to was the teaching of Abraham (Abraham-Hicks), my favorite Law of Attraction teacher. The Law of Attraction states that whatever you consistently think and believe, you draw into your own reality, therefore we have no creative power in someone else's reality.

Abraham states, *"The Law of Attraction, the most powerful Universal Law, is your friend. By the Universal Law of Attraction (that which is like unto itself is drawn), you are attracting the essence of whatever you are giving your attention to—wanted or unwanted."*

I learned from Abraham that in order to reach your goals, you must be energetically aligned in your mind, body, and soul. I realized why I didn't accomplish certain goals - I wasn't energetically aligned.

I was vibrating on a low frequency and spent my thought energy focusing on the absence of the goal instead of feeling and visualizing how it would be to have my heart's desires.

One of my favorite quotes from Abraham states *"Action does not create. Your vibrational offering of thought Energy produces the results that you live. If you will take the time to line up your Energy, meaning create a vibrational match between your desire and your belief, the Universe will deliver to you amazing circumstances and events toward your physical conclusions.*

However, if you proceed with action before you have aligned your Energies of belief and desire; there is not enough action in the world to make any real difference.

Once you learn to align with the Energy of your Source you will discover that action is not a key ingredient to the fulfillment of your desires for abundance, success, joy or any other physical fulfillment. Line up your Energy and then follow the inspired action and you will live happily ever after."

In their book, '*Ask and It Is Given*' they offer several processes on how to align your energy to reach your goals.

Some shifts began happening to me. My new beliefs are:

1. Whenever I come to the table, I bring value.
2. I deserve success.
3. My writing is stimulating and exciting, serves humanity and rewards me financially.

Nothing has ever changed about my writing. I still believe I am an awesome and memorable writer. Kristi did a free teleclass and featured Mary Foley, one of the authors of '*Bodacious! An AOL Insider Cracks the Code to Outrageous Success for Women.*'

That class inspired me to be more bodacious! Kristi stressed that what you focus on will expand in your life and that becomes your reality. She also had Dr. Roberta Shaler, a coach and author of '*What You Pay Attention to Expands—Focus Your Thinking, Change Your Results*', speak to our group.

Now I pay strict attention to what I am thinking about. I will no longer have randomly negative thoughts floating in my head such as:

- I hate my life.
- I wish I were anybody but me.
- I never get what I want.
- I can't win.
- I am the stupidest person I know.
- Life is a struggle.
- Life is tricky.
- I never get ahead.
- I am not well-connected.
- I am operating from a place of disadvantage.
- My life as an ant sucks.
- I don't have enough money.

I now have enough tools to guide myself through any situation. Because I really can't afford the luxury of a negative thought, doesn't mean I don't have challenges. I ask Spirit and my angels to help me daily, and they do.

One of the biggest events that impacted my life was when Kristi turned us on to *"Coachville"*, and I did the clean sweep questionnaire. I also read over their 1000 tolerations list and declared no more tolerating the things I don't want.

My most favorite thing Kristi turned us on to was the seven energy systems in the body, known as the chakras. I even had several private coaching sessions with Kristi to help understand my chakras system. I encourage you to check out all the websites because they are all packed with resources to help inspire and motivate you. She turned us on to so many resources that I have enough information to coach myself; however, I still recommend a coach. I could even write a book about my experience.

I must confess, this wasn't easy because I was making a paradigm shift. My old beliefs, which I had for years and negative culture beliefs were being challenged and uprooted by new beliefs. For a second, try to imagine uprooting a tree by hand that's been planted for thirty-five years or centuries. How many years do you think it would take? I would encourage people on this journey to be patient and gentle with them. Get clear about what you want, allow it to come into your life, and remember the law of detachment.

Get a coach!! To learn more about how a coach can help you manifest the life your heart truly desires, go to websites such as; www.coachville.com, www.teleclass.com, www.coachu.com or any of the other websites I've mentioned.

The best compliment Kristi gave me was, *"I am really proud of you because you're willing to do the work to improve your life."* The best part about this group was Kristi. She was our lead *"Diva Coach."* She has a great nurturing spirit. In addition, I was getting group coaching and learning so much from everyone else's wisdom and stories.

That was the plus of the group. I'm so grateful for all of my WE Success Sisters. The most powerful tool Coach Kristi reminded me about was having an attitude of gratitude. As a result, I resumed keeping my daily gratitude journal, instead of taking my blessings for granted.

Carolyn Myss states, *"We evolve at a rate consistent with the group that we are plugged into."* I am so grateful I was plug into this group.

Though the season for our WE Success Group has ended, I have to say, I love you Kristi; you're my angelic coach. I have so much to thank you for, especially the rebirth of Cleopatra Bell, because like Cleopatra's of the past, this Cleopatra was born to reign, too.

P.S. So were you!

~~~~~~
CLEOPATRA Bell, Distinguished Toastmaster, Artistic Coach, Keynote Speaker, Workshop Leader, and Author of '*Be A Thriving Artist, Not A Starving Artist*'.
~~~~~~

Letting Go Of The Pain
Georgina - Australia

I believe life is a continual journey of change; it is what we do when we feel the winds of change that determine the outcome of that particular season of our lives.

This particular journey began when I was twenty years old. I was working until 5am in a nightclub, drinking a lot, smoking marijuana, taking a mixture of different drugs; speed, acid, ecstasy - sometimes all at the same time depending on what was readily available and I was involved with many different men.

My life consisted of loud music, late nights/early mornings and most of my time was spent out of it on drugs.

One night my friends and I were at my house and I decided I would take a little more ecstasy than I usually took, I was a little disappointed that I wasn't getting the intense high I expected so I also took some acid along with it.

It was a weird kind of feeling I experienced - nothing like I thought it would be - I stayed in my room most of the night totally paranoid - quite uneventful really. I went to sleep and woke up totally disoriented and very scared. I couldn't walk so I crawled to my room mate's room, woke her up and asked her if she knew what was happening to me. She said, "*Don't worry about it, its normal.*"

Wake up call #1 - THIS WAS NOT NORMAL.

I crawled into the bathroom where I lay on the cold tile floor for a long time. Still unable to get a grip I managed to drag myself into the bathtub where I felt a little more secure because I was still feeling the cold from the tub and was surrounded on three sides.

The feeling eventually passed but I was left with an uneasy feeling and I was beginning to see the way I was living was not good. But I didn't stop.

I'm not sure whether this was during one of the two nights mentioned above or not but I woke up from another wild and crazy night and went to the bathroom.

I looked in the mirror, what or who I saw in the mirror scared me - who had I become - who is this person looking back at me.

I asked myself - "*why won't you let me be happy*" - "*who are you*". I was scared and it took me a long time before I would look at myself in the mirror again.

Wake up call #2 - WHERE WAS GEORGIE.

Things were not going well between my room mate and I so I moved back home. Because of the distance I would have to travel to my job in the nightclub from where my mum lived I had to leave my job.

I went back to office work and took a part time job in the local pub. It wasn't long after I moved home I found out the man I was seeing, a drug dealer, had been caught dealing drugs in Queensland and was in jail.

Well, I freaked out, took a shower, got dressed and went back to the nightclub I used to work at and got completely plastered, ended up throwing up and having to be taken back to a friend's place where I started to smoke some marijuana - not a good idea.

I started to lose my grip - now it was my friends turn to hold my hand and walk me through some tough hours. The next day I began walking and kept walking until I ended up at the drug dealer's house.

The door was boarded up by the police so I went to a friend of his up the street and stayed there for the rest of the day, smoking cigarettes and talking. I went back to the house I shared with my room mate and stayed there for a couple of days until the drug dealer was released on bail.

I picked him up and took him back to my old house, lent him my car to get around doing some things and then finding out he was seeing a lot of other women as well as me. I was devastated.

During this time I was so stressed I didn't eat anything, just smoked a lot of cigarettes and fretted. I had done something to my stomach and I couldn't keep anything in - it would go straight through me.

I lost a lot of weight and was not healthy. I didn't go to doctors so I went to a naturopath and he gave me some herbs and told me to eat soup and stop smoking, drinking etc.

Wake up call #3 – I'M UPSIDE DOWN

So, I did, I gave everything up - smoking, drinking, drugs and the drug dealer - totally cold turkey. It was not an easy journey; I had been drinking and smoking heavily since I was 15 years old so I really didn't know how to function without it.

My life was so turned upside down by all these events so, in a way I was forced to change or continue to deteriorate.

I continued to eat well and stay off drugs and alcohol but I was now totally lost and alone. All my friends were still living the lifestyle I had left behind and I didn't know what to do with myself.

The journey continued right into becoming involved in the new age movement called "*Mind Powers*" where I found out there was a spiritual world, where I learned to look after my body and live a healthy life. I devoured all their teachings, I bought all the books, listened to all the tapes and did all the exercises to be the person I wanted to be - a healer.

I saw visions and experienced a very active spiritual world. During this time I had given up on men - they had only brought me heartache. I had become very close to an also ex-girlfriend of the drug dealer I had been seeing earlier.

I began desiring a relationship with this woman. One night after a party I was staying at her house and I decided I would make my move - ha, she fell asleep.

The next day, I woke up without an alarm clock, got off the pool table - where we were sleeping and went to church. That day I gave my life to Jesus and haven't turned back. All of this happened in one year.

Now I look back on this journey and I am so thankful for God's guiding hand. I wasn't aware of it at the time but God was there during every step.

Georgie's Poem of Change

The exhilaration of the wind in my sails,
Powering at a rapid speed.
The water parting either side of my pointed bow.
An assurance of a sturdy keel
Holding me steady.
Liberated and excited above,
My mouth the rudder.

My whole direction could change
By one seemingly mere word
So much power beholds the tongue
The tongue says gybe (jibe) after the wind has altered
We yield and go with the flow
Or fight and gain no ground

The choice is yours...

My Name Is Aaron
Andy - USA

MY NAME IS ANDY; MY NAME IS AARON, for I am both. In an attempt to solidify my identity, both within myself and in the world, I decided to drop the nickname my mother had tagged me with, Andy, and instead fully embrace my given, legal name; Aaron. I would cease being Andy, and completely become Aaron. It was like a reverse name change.

I informed everyone I knew that I was dropping my nickname Andy, and to please call me Aaron from now on. No one really understood what I was trying to accomplish – and I'm not sure I can put it into words. I was just trying to identify with my biological father, by accepting his name as my own.

People at work started calling me Aaron, as did my friends, people at my church, and even my family started coming around to doing this. It didn't happen overnight, and it was not easy. It was hard enough to explain to spiritual people, who knew the many stories of how God changed names in the Bible.

For instance, God changed Abram's name to Abraham, and Sari's name to Sarah, Jacob to Israel, and so forth. Jesus often changed people's names also. He renamed Simon as Peter. He called the brothers, James and John, the sons of Zebedee (their fathers name), to the sons of thunder. The bible is packed full of one account after another where people's names were changed. Just think of Saul become Paul in the New Testament. Easy, Simple, Biblical, Sound; the precedence had already been set.

After around eight months after this name change, most people had gotten used to calling me Aaron, with the exception of my wife. She had a difficult time with it. In fact, I think she thought I was nuts. I just wanted to identify with my father, and taking his name, the name I was given at birth, my legal name, was a way to do that and establish my new, true identity.

Then it came to a head. So many people did not understand. I didn't have the words, nor the desire, to explain the lifetime of frustration of having two different names, one 'real', and the other like an alias, an 'also-known-as' name. I was exasperated and frustrated.

Then, one day in my study, my wonderful study, my fortress of solitude, my place where I studied the Word, prayed and talked to God, worshiped and fellowshipped with Him, that I just lost it. Aaron? Andy? Aaron? Andy? Aaron? Andy...... No, this wasn't Schizophrenia. There were no hallucinations and delusions. It was just a good old fashion identify crisis.

It then occurred to me that I had never heard God my Father address me by either of these names. I stood upright in my study, for I had been on my knees praying, lifted my hands and eyes toward heaven, and called out my question to Him. "Father God, what do you call me?"

There was a long pause of silence.........

"*I call you son*", was His only reply.

And then the miracles began.

A Chance To Coach
Bobby – USA

The most significant change in my life and profession was when I changed living in my hometown to living in a town I had never heard of to take a job at a college I knew nothing about.

I was born in Birmingham, Alabama, went to grammar school, high school and Howard College located in Birmingham. My first coaching job, after graduation in 1953, was as Assistant Football and Head Track Coach at Howard College therefore the first 25 years of my life were spent in Birmingham.

In 1955 I was offered the Head Football Coach and Athletic Directors job at South Georgia College. I was 25 years old; my wife Ann was 22 years old. We had three children and were expecting a fourth.

The question was after living in Birmingham for 25 years; being in the presence of both our parents, should we pick up and leave the security and comfort we had in Birmingham to go to a small, rural Georgia community 300 miles away?

Ann and I prayed about it and felt it was an opportunity and chance one had to take. Our first football team at South Georgia College won the Georgia State Junior College Championship and after 4 successful years I was offered the head football coaching job at Samford University.

This led me to head coaching jobs at West Virginia University and Florida State University. After 55 years of college coaching, I guess me and my family moving to Douglas, Georgia was the correct change!

~~~~~~

Coach Bobby Bowden
Head Football Coach, Florida State University
~~~~~~

Making A Full Shift
Mark – USA

After reading *'The Shack'* and the "*constant E-mails*" from a friend of mine, I will now sit for a time and relate to my friends and family the moment that impacted me and caused a "*shift*" in me and the way I see and live life.

Scrolling back over the years I'd have to say the first ten years of my marriage to my sweet wife were less than pristine. We were both so immature and looking for what we could get out of the marriage, not what we could put into it. We had some friends that tried to help but stubbornness prevented the input to sink in. I was too busy tripping through the minefields of life to look at the big picture.

I had become a Christian on July 4, 1976. Isn't it neat how God meets you and grabs my life on a date that means so much to a history buff like me! But touching my heart and capturing my spirit at that point were worlds apart, until May of 1985. My life seemed simple, a loving wife, two great kids, good job and yet it all seemed to come crashing down around me.

During that time my wife was having severe headaches and the Doctors couldn't figure out why. At first they thought it was one thing and then another, I even wondered if it was me! Then as a last resort before sending her to get in touch with her emotions, they had a CT scan done to eliminate everything else and much to their surprise they found a growth.

We were both stunned when we were sent to one of the best local Neurosurgeons. Even though it seemed we were both floating those initial few days, we were relieved to finally know what was causing the problems. We were no longer running down any more rabbit trails.

During this time I went through a range of emotions; anger, frustration, fear, and an overwhelming sense of hopelessness (there's that word again). Looking back at it all, God met me during each time and gave me hope. A hope grounded in the fact that it was ok for me to feel these negative emotions I was going through as long as I didn't wallow in it.

My wife, during a quiet time in the hospital with God had an audible voice (God's) tell her that she was going to have a long life. We both grabbed hold of that and clung on for dear life. Looking back again it was good that God told her that and not that she was going to be healed. I think it helped us both to rest in the "*Goodness of God*" and block out all the whirlwind of things that were going on around us.

We prayed for the doctors and hospital staff and one such day while some of the doctors were out in the hall discussing my wife's condition, I went out, stood in the middle of them and told them we had every confidence in them because God had told us that my wife was going to have a long life.

I'm sure they thought I was some crazy Christian that didn't have all the "*facts*". As a side note, which is much more then a side note were our friends. There is no way I could have made it through any of this with out my friends. Having someone to laugh and cry with is the best example I can think of, of our Father's love for us here on earth.

I would have to say the way God carried me through this time and the after effect of it all has caused me to grow in ways I wouldn't have ever imagined.

Like the dad in the book "*The Shack*", I think I came out of this a better husband, father and man. I am more ready to tackle the things that God has set before me, trying not to sweat the little things in life and look at the bigger picture the way God does.

I'm more in love with my wife with each passing day and so proud of the girls he blessed me with. I'm a content man with a zest for each new and wonderful day!

The Country Lane
Rose – USA

There are many people that speak of change in how one perceives death and what existence might lie beyond our natural life. The following story is from Rose and how it changed her perception or attitude towards death.

Rose passed away late in the year of 2008, but her experience happened many years earlier. It was during this earlier time that she found peace in the dying process. Most certainly she was never in a hurry to die, but in the same breath she was not afraid of dying.

She was preceded in death by her father and a brother by the time this experience awakened her view. It is the "*seeing of a light*" in someone's dying eyes that you hear others speak about. Yet it is never something that we seem to experience as it is always happening to others.

This time it was her brother that lay in his final days of cancer. It was in a hospital room with his loving sister Rose by his bedside. She was there to comfort and encourage him in his final breath. For most of the time he lay quiet and sleeping with shallow movement.

At the moment of his final breath, he opened his eyes and she looked deep into them telling him how much she loved him. Over and over expressing her love for him, it was the vision of a country lane in his eyes. It was lined by beautiful trees and a most peaceful sight to behold.

It was this moment, a changing moment, she knew that death was not to be feared. It held her in good stead in later years. The death of a daughter, another brother and her own mother, each difficult but comforted by the experience given to her earlier.

A lane to walk peacefully down can change your life; it will comfort you in your own life.

Choice At The Crossroads Continues

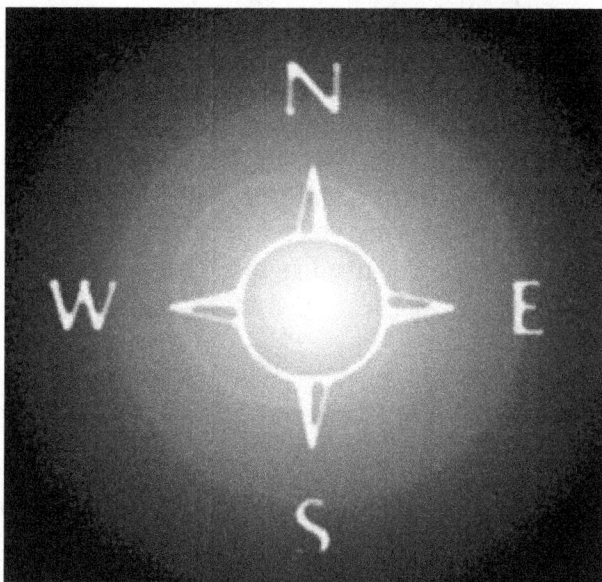

As one can tell from the previous stories, is that life is full of choices for us to pick from. You have to take that opportunity with your dreams and visions in your pocket. And which choice are you going to take? Is it to leave your hopes upon the wall and walk back down the same old path you have been over so many times?

Or will you decide upon change and step through that door of opportunity? It really is a simple question, choose to change or choose not to change. It is the making of that decision which can be so difficult.

For me, I was a middle aged man whom for years left his dreams upon the walls of the gathering room. It was a dreary place that I came to so often, only to shy away from the brightness that shined through that open door. With the others, I turned to walk back down that beaten and worn path. There were so many of us using a path that seemed at the time comforting.

Every day I would come to the building in my mind. The routine was to pick up my dreams and wait patiently for the appointed time. It was a time that when the door swung open wide with expectation and wonderment. Yet I always allowed stubborn reason to deny me.

I had been living life the same way for so many years. Why change now? What would be the point in disrupting the steady pace of life? Sure, there were many good things in my life with moments of greatness. Yet my life and the life of others around me in this building never seemed to rise to a new level.

There were many things I tried in life, some of which I became very successful at. It was a career that seemed to be moving forward with a promotion here and there. I tried different things to make money in order to feed what seemed to be an insatiable appetite that life had around my family.

I never seemed to understand that my own attitude towards life was more important then money in determining the quality of that life. It was in trying so hard that I felt I was slipping even further into nothing.

It was a number of years earlier that the building near the crossroads was brought to my attention by a friend. The friend had talked of life changing possibility by simply walking through an open door. Similar to others around me, the idea excited my senses and of how easy it was supposed to be.

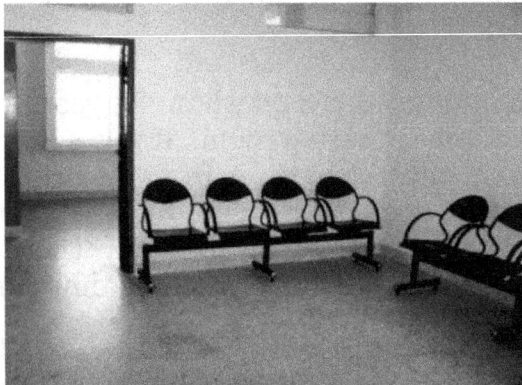

It was much later that I decided to go and see what it was all about. When I first entered the room, it looked like any other room such as a dreary waiting room at the Department of Motor Vehicles. But a slight difference in atmosphere did exist.

Many people were excited and moved about the room in hushed voices. Many were talking to others and to themselves for that matter. Their conversations spoke of what was on the other side, to what will happen to those left behind.

Eventually I could hear people turn their talk to questioning if this was a good idea at all. They spoke of doubt on the goodness that lay beyond '*the door*'. It made me wonder what I would do the moment that door opened. Could I step boldly through?

And then I did see the door open; the light that shown in was so clear, so vibrant. It took me aback, startling me into a dumb silence. All of my current life circled in my mind. I began to wonder if it was such a good thing to leave it all behind. The life I was living wasn't so bad, why change now?

With out announcement, the door closed and the dull gray light took over the room once again. I was startled again to finally notice how dreary this room truly was. The open door had revealed the difference and I knew I would have to return the next day.

And every day I did return to see the light of possibility shine through that open door. And every day I hesitated to walk through the open door. There were always reasons for not moving forward in my life.

What would my friends say; what if I failed; what was really out there? I allowed myself to listen to others in that room. They were the naysayers that were never going to walk through the door. I had supposed their only purpose was to keep others from walking through that door of opportunity. Today they remind me of all the negative people I had allowed to surround myself with. That is not a good idea when you are trying to move forward in life. To succeed you need to surround yourself with successful and positive people.

I had not yet learned that lesson and had believed these other people had good reasons. I allowed myself to accept what it was they said. From time to time I would argue in defense of the life that I wanted. That would almost get me through the door. But I always allowed the others to hold me back. So together we would go back down the weary old path once the door had closed for the day.

Thinking back on it, all I had to do was walk through an open door. It didn't require me to unlock it, turn a handle or push it open. Someone was there to simply open it for me to walk through. Why was something so easy, so difficult to do?

And then something changed.....

"The greatest discovery of my generation is that a human being can change his life by changing his attitude of mind."
William James

Upon returning home one afternoon, my house appeared much more quiet then normal. Through the living room to the dining room and kitchen one could tell people lived here. There was proof of existence but yet no one to be found. For an hour I sat in the quiet of the house, contemplating what had become of my life. Darkness had fallen when the lights of a car pulled into the driveway casting long shadows through out the house.

My wife had returned from some place, I couldn't remember where it was she had said. Think, what was it she had told me early that morning; the memory just wasn't there. When entering the darkened house, she began to turn on the lights, startled to find me there in the darkness. There were the pleasant exchanges of *'how was your day'* but no warmness. We were two boats upon the water drifting steadily apart.

I asked where the kids were and she reminded me of what she said to me that morning. None of what she said could be remembered. Was I living life on auto-pilot, letting the world around me drift by while I worked so hard to provide for them? My family was floating away and I was starting to see the last traces of my current life.

There are many different outcomes to trouble within a marriage or family. Some are able to work through and resolve those issues; able to get the help needed to correct the wrongs.

Yet others end up in divorce with the complications associated with such a decision. Each choice is an avenue to a solution, but it is how one conducts oneself through the process that will determine the level of pain and amount of recovery needed.

In my marriage, it was a number of things that set us adrift from each other. What hurt most was a secret relationship she had developed with another. It was one of the hardest things emotionally that you can go through. The one that you have devoted your life to and had been most intimate with simply turned a switch off, namely me.

During this period of my life, everything seemed to collapse around me. I kept trying to hold it all together, work, home, friends as well as the marriage. You go through this stage in which you believe it can be fixed. You tell yourself that if you just try to keep everything normal, all will be well.

The problem is that you are actually fighting a new normal. Things have changed and what you are holding onto is no longer reality but I kept trying. Then the story of my neighbor's dog changed my view of reality.

I have always had a *'people pleasing'* type of personality. So in *'keeping it all together'*, I would accommodate other people's needs even in the midst of a major personal issue. As it is, I agreed to watch after our long time neighbor's dogs. They were going on a short vacation and I felt it would be something *'normal'* to do. Again, *'normal'* to someone going through a crisis is not *'reality'*.

These dogs were interesting dogs to say the least. One was a mid-sized dog, full of excitement and would do anything the older dog did. The older dog was a Beagle and if you know anything about them, they like to be adventurous. There was no fence high enough, secure enough or *'Beagle-proof'* enough to keep that dog at home.

So many times this dog would get out; the younger and more impressionable *'dog-pal'* would follow along. Someone would find them not too far away, read the dog tag and bring them home. An *'invisible'* dog fence with collar never seemed to deter these dogs either.

My hands would be full but it was a way to feel *'normal'*. So I took on the job and figured, *"what could go wrong?"* It didn't take long and at the end of the first day, my son called and said that the dogs were out running about. A Good Samaritan brought them home and what should they do with them? Put them in our garage and I'll deal with it when I get home from work is what I said. The excitement was just about to begin.

I arrived home with a storm dumping rain about 5:30 in the evening. Both dogs were in our garage and excited at seeing me; wasn't I the lucky one? This was nothing abnormal so I took them back home, fed them and left them on their own. Things were different at my home and making supper for the boys was next on the list.

The next day, a repeat of the previous day's events had me a bit more agitated. The dogs were excited to see me upon my arrival home from their adventure out and about during the day. This time I wasn't thinking nearly as clearly. With the rain falling down upon me, both dogs were on leashes as I started back across the street.

For some reason, the metal chain-link leash for the larger dog was wrapped around my hand and a shorter leash on the smaller dog. We came across the front lawn of their home and I had forgotten about the 'invisible' fence. Those wonderful devices that work in conjunction with a collar that delivers a small shock that teaches them not to cross a certain point.

I had forgotten about that as I marched the dogs to their back yard area. The larger dog excitedly made his way across the yard and got the impact of the invisible fence. Off he went in one direction and the Beagle, older and smarter refused to budge. As the metal chain dug deeper into my hand, it was now or never and across the yard I finally pulled the Beagle.

The mind has a way of playing with you under times of duress and this was one of them. I was going to outsmart the Beagle and figure out a way not to let this dog get out again. If the Beagle doesn't get out, the larger dog stays put.

So I decided to place the dog house up on the large sprawling deck and chain the dog close to it. With food and water near by, all should go well as I went back home to make supper. I had outsmarted the dog and could concentrate on other things.

I made a quick check on the dogs the next morning and then was off to work. It was a full day that really wasn't normal but I was hanging onto what I thought was reality. With no phone calls from my boys, I was proud of outsmarting the Beagle.

But when I arrived home, the larger and much more animated dog was running around his front yard. There was no Beagle to be seen in this almost surreal scene that was starting to unfold in front of me. Where was the Beagle and why was the larger dog out? My reality was about to take a dose of 'real' reality.

The large dog was easy enough to corral and head towards the back yard. Calling out for the Beagle in hopes she would be quietly sitting on the back deck was met with something entirely different. As I rounded the corner, I found the chain stretched out across the deck to the stairs.

In my attempt to protect the dog, I had left the chain about six inches too short or two feet too long. I say this with all sympathy and pain that the dog had accidently come off the edge of the porch and hung itself. A lifeless dog caused by me, both of us in the pouring rain; was this the new reality?

I called my neighbor and explained the situation. All was okay with the situation and he only had one request for me to which I fully agreed. This was to bury the dog out at the back of the property, the dog facing outward towards the fence in one last symbol of the nature of Beagles.

So here I am in my new reality, rain pouring down in the gathering darkness of night, burying a Beagle. Mud and wetness filling my entire being and the weight of it all finally awoke me to the reality of my life. My marriage had disintegrated and I felt all of life was falling in around me. Everything I had worked so hard for was gone. There was no way that I was going to be able to hold onto any of it.

Where and what should I do now as I gathered a six-pack of beer and headed to my own back deck to drink myself blind. And there I was, sitting in the pouring rain, drinking and talking to myself; talking to the inner voice inside of me. But who was that voice that kept speaking back to me. I wondered if it was God all along and figured that I might as well talk as though it were.

Self pity and grand depression were taking hold of me at this point. After four or five beers, there is no inhibition to talking out load. So I asked, *"okay, what more do you want from me?"* In the depths of depression, lack of self worth and pain, I was demanding an answer from my inner voice.

It was at that moment everything changed. The one thing I didn't expect was a response and all I can remember hearing is, *"your love."* Those words were as loud and clear as two people talking to each other on the street. It was an eye opening experience that I point to as my moment of *'change.'*

It is amusing how we tend to find God in the depths of pain. The cynic may say it is our last gasp effort to find God. I figure that during good times we just fail to see him through all of the haze of our humanness. God is always there and not just during the good times.

What I had forgotten was the meaning in giving to those around me. It wasn't about the money and things, but about my God, my family, my friends and I. Now what was I going to do, where should I go from this point of change?

Even the momentary light of *'the door'* didn't seem to warm me anymore. Was this the end or just the beginning? Change brings a whole new unknown into the equation of your life. For many days I didn't return to building near the crossroads. There seemed to be no point in going for I finally felt that my lot in life had been cast. I would sit in darkened rooms thinking about this change in my life. It was a new reality that I now had to deal with.

Just because something changes in our life does not mean it will be easy. But during all of this time, that small voice inside of my head kept speaking to me. Even though I took it to be God that was speaking, a part of me thought I was crazy. And at times I really did think I was going a bit crazy hearing the words inside.

After many more days of self pity, I began to think more about those words I had heard. *'Your Love'* were the words that kept replaying in my mind and I eventually began to place myself back out among other people.

I started to reconnect with those that I called real friends and trusted with their honesty. My faith in many things had been lost and shaken, but I knew it was necessary to find a way back from this deep valley. Slowly I sought help as I realized that a point had been reached that doing it alone was not possible.

Faith and belief in a better life started to become a possibility, a dim light of expectation. This also caused the voice inside of me to grow even louder. So I learned all there was to know about what had happened in my life.

It was a truthful look inside and the events that had placed me at this moment in time, which was an eye opening experience. Even though others had a share in the situation, I knew that to take responsibility for my own attitude, my own life was the necessary thing to do.

Without grabbing hold of a new way of thinking, a new way of approaching life, I could not move to a better life. I began to shed the '*victim*' mentality and accepted a new attitude. As the days passed, I even returned to the building by the crossroads. Possibility was once again in my heart and mind.

Then it happened as it does to everyone that chooses to change. For some it is a chance encounter, to others it is a friend making a suggestion. It comes in many different forms and not always as a bolt of lightening. Many times it is a subtle change of wind that causes us to take that next step.

From that moment of change, in the pouring rain in the depths of sorrow, my path was now brought back to this door of opportunity.

"And I stepped through the open door."

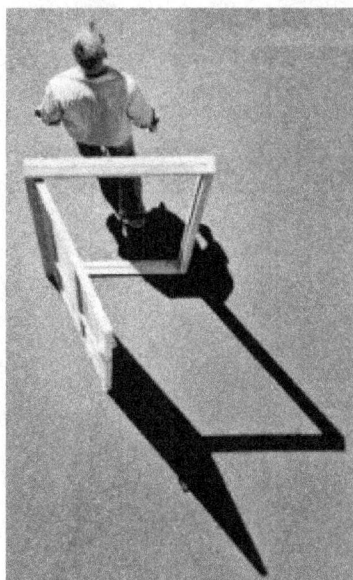

It was out into a bright and vibrant sky with roads leading many different ways. Which one should I take? But I knew the answer already. Any one of the roads would be fine for if one didn't work out, there were always others. Always other answers, other possibilities and a life full of opportunity. For I had a new attitude and life was going to be great.

Change will occur sometimes with you and sometimes without you. It is how you deal with that change or how you make change that will determine the level of life. Wallow in despair and that is where you will stay. Accept change and make movement in your life.

Take down your dreams and visions from the wall and place them into your pocket. Then take a step to walk through the door and out onto the crossroads. Choose a path and know that whatever you do, failure or success, is that change is always possible. This means that possibility is endless.

> *"If you don't know where you are going,*
> *any road will get you there."*
> Lewis Carroll

Making a choice when you come to a crossroads is not always an easy thing to do. You look down each road and wonder which to take. You stand there faced with only three real choices; choose a path, stand where you are forever or go back to where you came from.

I decided to change my life and am now happily remarried for a number of years. Much happier, much more focused and much more understanding of what life has to offer each of us.

When you make that choice which places you at the crossroads, choose any one of the roads and let change take place. If you find the choice isn't right, you can always change. That's the great thing, change can take place.

Life is full of choices for us to pick from. But you have to take that opportunity with your dreams and visions in your pocket. Which choice are you going to take? To leave your hopes upon the wall, walking back down the same old path you've been over so many times.

Or will you decide upon change, to step through that door. It's a simple question, choose to change or choose not to change.

"I have made decisions that turned out to be wrong, and went back and did it another way, and still took less time than many who procrastinated over the original decision."
Jerry Gillies

Choose change, choose now, you won't regret it. To chase your dreams, you will catch them.

Where The Road Continues

When change occurs in our life, the road ahead becomes much clearer. The time and events leading up to that moment of change are not lost. They are life learning events that we simply had to work ourselves through.

All of the stories you have read here are incomplete. The people whose lives were impacted by change are still on their journey. The exception you might feel is that of Rose. Even though Rose has passed away, she is on a different kind of journey.

One can also argue that her experience lives on inside of anyone that has heard her story. Like the pebble dropped in the water, the resultant wave radiates out and touches many others.

My own story doesn't end simply by walking through that door in the building near the crossroads. By stepping out in change, I was presented with possibility. The path ahead of me was still there, but it started to come into focus.

I was presented with opportunity and new found hope. But the idea that it was all easy is the farthest from the truth. The road can still be difficult and full of choices. It is those new choices that give us optimism to see a clearer future.

It was more then apparent to me that divorce was the beginning of this journey. My former wife had already moved on to her new life with another. I had accepted that I could no longer trust a relationship with her. So one of us had to finally make the decision, which I did and twenty-one years of marriage ended. I feel certain she is happy in her new life.

The road for me was difficult both emotionally and from all of the other adjustments one has to make. Others around us had to adjust as well, namely our children. Life after divorce was certainly not the change they would have expected in their lives. But change can come whether you create it or not.

Change occurred and the '*ripple*' effect flowed out to all of the people around us. It is how you choose to deal with those '*ripple*' effects and the '*backwash*' it will create. My former wife and I made a decision to make this as amicable as possible and to keep the kids first in our thoughts.

Other changes occurred and I began to give thought to moving on to another relationship. I was introduced to a very nice woman by a co-worker. It came at a time when I wasn't fully ready to even think about meeting someone new. But as my friend and I sat eating wings and having a beer, he simply asked if I would like to go see a movie. It would be nothing big; he, his wife and her sister along with me to see a simple movie.

I could accept or say no to this offer. All I could see was another door that was opening. It was one that I didn't expect or go looking for, so I told him I'd think about it over night. I went home and did just that. I was 41-years old and certainly thought no, then yes and then again no. Then the light of that opening door seemed to start fading.

The next morning I saw my friend and simply told him, *"that thing we talked about last night, yes, I will come along."* And with that my life began to change once again.

We met and all went for dinner and a movie. *"The Princess Diaries"* was not a movie I would have thought a great date movie, but it turned out to be perfect in retrospect. We fell in love and began to work through the idea of combining a family of my four boys and her four girls.

Ten months after first meeting, we married in what was a great and wonderful moment in my life. A most beautiful bride, all of our friends and family close by; it was fantastic to say the least.

Did the road end there? No, the scenery changed and the wind may have shifted, but most of all, it was good.

> *To exist is to change, to change is to mature,*
> *to mature is to go on creating oneself endlessly.*
> Henri Louis Bergson

Each of us moves from one moment in life to the next. We continuously change and adjust to the circumstance and general whims that life seems to place in front of us. It is how we react to circumstances which will dictate the everyday of our lives.

By stepping out in faith, we give ourselves the opportunity to discover new and greater things. One might find that change is a reason to give up on what one already has in favor of something different. That is far from what the message of this book is about.

Change is about seeking something far greater for everything in your life. For my life, the mother of my boys apparently found that she needed change from me. I wouldn't want to speak for her decision, but it forced me to examine my own life. It was in that which I discovered my ability to put away the fear of change. Once I boldly stepped through that door, life became clear and in focus.

You get to face change in your life and it is the decision that you make which matters. We either stay in one place, stagnant and miserable. Or we choose to step forward, through the door of change into a greater life.

It is you that has to make that decision – choose the open door.

CONCLUSION

There really is no conclusion to the story. Each of us continues to create and define our journey. Each of the people that have shared their experience only wants the best in life for you.

By reading how others changed their lives, it provides courage and strength for you to do the same. If only one word moved only one person for the better, then I feel all of the work creating this book was worth it.

The journey of change is not easy, it is not fast and it is not going to accomplish everything you want. But the journey is there regardless of whether you participate or not. Why not make the most of it? Each of us has the capacity inside to accomplish greatness, if only we have the faith and courage to step through the open door.

Create change in your life. I have faith in your ability as do many other people. If all of us know that you can do it, then surely you can have faith in yourself.

~~

THE END, WHICH IS JUST A BEGINNING

~~

Strength, Belief and Embrace

Stand strong through your hard times
and know you can change your circumstances.

Keep believing in your visions and dreams
when others try to destroy your belief.

Embrace all that you are.

About the Author

Joseph Primm is a person like most anyone else you may have met on the street. Since 1980, he has worked in the technology field at a Fortune 500 firm where he spends days resolving technical and customer issues.

He describes himself as a simple farm boy from Nebraska that married young, has four boys and four step-daughters that bring him joy and inspiration. His loving wife Laura continues to provide the support and inspiration for his books.

Having learned many important lessons through life's ups and downs, he has devoted his spare time to writing a daily online web blog. His goal is to share those lessons learned so that they will be a source of motivation and inspiration to others.

These same articles serve as the content for his series of books called "Attitude In Words", which is also meant to inspire and motivate others into greatness.

While not a professional writer or motivational speaker, Joseph simply wants to provide an extra bit of encouragement to others. By speaking to others, writing a daily web blog and publishing books, he is intent on helping others improve their lives.

Published works;

Attitude In Words, © 2008   ISBN 978-1-4357-1582-0

www.ingramcontent.com/pod-product-compliance
Lightning Source LLC
Chambersburg PA
CBHW031522040426
42445CB00009B/346